The Farmer's Crop

By Andrew Abel

Illustrations by Carolyn Chaffee Li

Copyright © 2022 Andrew Abel

All rights reserved.

ISBN: 979-8-9883394-0-3

DEDICATION

From Andrew
For Madison, Melia, Luke & Rocky

From Carolyn
For Zoe

CONTENTS

	Acknowledgments	i
1	The Crow	2
2	The Path	4
3	The Hedgerow	6
4	Ground Fallow	8
5	Water Flows	10
6	Share His Love	12

ACKNOWLEDGMENTS

I want to thank Carolyn for the beautiful block print illustrations. I would also like to thank Angela Abel, Catherine Clarke and Marie Chaffee for proof reading and general advice about my poetry and book publishing.

The Farmer's Crop

by Andrew Abel

1 THE CROW

The farmer wants
his crops to grow.
He enters the field
to sow, sow, sow.

And spreads the seed
wherever it can go.
But a black bird swoops in
low, low, low,
And the seed's carried off
by a big fat crow.

2 THE PATH

The farmer wants
his crops to grow.
He enters the field
to sow, sow, sow.

But the seed falls onto
the path below.
On dry dirt there's
no room to grow,
So the roots are short
and too shallow.

3 THE HEDGEROW

The farmer wants
his crops to grow.
He enters the field
to sow, sow, sow

And spreads the seed
in the old hedgerow,
Where the weeds and brambles
often grow,
And choke the grain
as the east winds blow.

4 GROUND FALLOW

The farmer wants
his crops to grow.
He enters the field
to sow, sow, sow.

And some seed falls on
ground fallow,
And digs its roots in
deep below,
And bears its fruit
a hundredfold.

5 WATER FLOWS

So heed the word
that the Father sows.
Listen close
to the One who knows.

In softened hearts
the seedling grows.
Not caught and choked
by wealth or woes,
It drinks in deep
where the water flows.

6 SHARE HIS LOVE

For it's God that wants
His life to grow,
And calls us all
to sow, sow, sow.

With childlike faith
and patience slow,
To plant a seed
and watch it grow,
And share His love
with those we know.

ABOUT THE AUTHOR

Andrew Abel is originally from Cheshire, England, but now lives in Silicon Valley, California with his wife, Angela. He developed a love of spoken rhyme from his grandfather, Wilfred Harrison, who loved to recite poems.

Andrew is proud to be grandpa to Madison, Melia, Luke & Rocky

ABOUT THE ILLUSTRATOR

Carolyn Chaffee Li is an artist residing with her husband Ray Li in the San Francisco Bay Area. Inspired by nature, her artwork is often about light and the metaphors it embodies. She enjoys experimenting with various mediums to portray light in meaningful ways. Her desire is to create artwork that conveys beauty, truth, and hope. She received her BA in Illustration and Studio Art from Seattle Pacific University. Her artwork has been profiled in several publications and exhibited in Seattle, New York, and the SF Bay Area.

Awards:

2022—Honorable Mention, Sunnyvale Art Club, 2022 Juried Art Exhibit

2021—1st Place, Gold Section, Sunnyvale Art Club competition

Website: http://www.carolynchaffee.com

Instagram: @carolynchaffeeart

www.ingramcontent.com/pod-product-compliance
Lightning Source LLC
Chambersburg PA
CBHW042011060526
44119CB00111B/196